Contents

A small tavern once situated off Catherine Street became known as The Whistling Oyster because the proprietor of the day, one Mr Pearkes, heard an unusual sound coming from one of the tubs of oysters, or rather, one oyster in particular.
The oyster concerned achieved a celebrity status of which some modern contemporaries can only dream, but its eventual fate remains unknown...

ISBN no. 978-0-9528644-3-1

Foreword
An introduction to Covent Garden's fascinating history

Seven Dials

The Central Market at Christmas time from the Royal Opera House terrace

Covent Garden has long been associated with entertainment and leisure; it is famous for its shops, street performers, arts and crafts, eating places, theatres and the Royal Opera House.

Built by the fourth Earl of Bedford in 1631 it has at its centre, an Italian-style piazza, London's first residential square, *"fit for the habitacions of Gentlemen and men of ability"*. In the 18th and 19th centuries, its reputation was tarnished by the coffee houses and taverns which sprang up together with shady lodging houses and brothels. Although disreputable, it was, as it is today, one of the liveliest parts of the capital.

At the heart of the piazza lies the famous market, now visited by millions of tourists each year, a far cry from its humble origins as a kitchen garden used by monks. Covent Garden went on to serve as the largest fruit and vegetable market in England until it was relocated in 1974.

Covent Garden today is alive and vibrant, buzzing with atmosphere, which makes it a place so beloved of Londoners and visitors alike. Jugglers, mime artists, musicians and variety acts amuse and delight the crowds. The very essence of the place owes much to its rich history and the colourful characters who have helped shape it. Over the centuries, the famous and the infamous together with heaving crowds of Londoners have walked the streets, watched plays, drunk coffee and ale, wined and dined, bought and sold, just as they do today.

The Market owes a great deal of its present character to *Covent Garden Area Trust* and the *Covent Garden Community Association*. Both set up in the 1970s/80s in response to the GLC's (Greater London Council) plans to redevelop the land, the organizations still actively represent the community and stand sentinel against any unsympathetic re-development of what is undoubtedly one of London's most lustrous gems.

The Naming of Covent Garden
Once the kitchen garden of the Benedictine Abbey

'Covent Garden' is actually a corruption of 'the Convent Garden', so named because the area had been owned by the Benedictine Abbey (or Convent) of St. Peter at Westminster since 969AD. It was bordered by what is now Long Acre to the north, with St. Martins Lane to the west, Drury Lane to the east and an irregular line parallel to the Strand to the south.

The actual convent garden is first documented in around 1200AD, consisting of about 40 acres of mainly pastureland with an enclosed central part. It was used as a kitchen garden for the Abbot and the monks of Westminster where they were able to grow produce such as apples, pears, plums, barley and other grains, as well as pasturing livestock to supply their daily food. Any surplus foodstuffs were sold in local markets to provide income for the Abbey.

Excavations in 1829 revealed large numbers of human bones, suggesting that the Abbots of Westminster also used part of the site as a burial place for the convent.

The garden was tended by the monks until around 1407 and was subsequently taken over by a variety of leaseholders, with the permission of the Abbot of Westminster.

Plan of Westminster from Nordens Survey 1593. Covent Garden is shown and St Martins-in-the-Fields can be seen directly above 'Charinge Crosse'

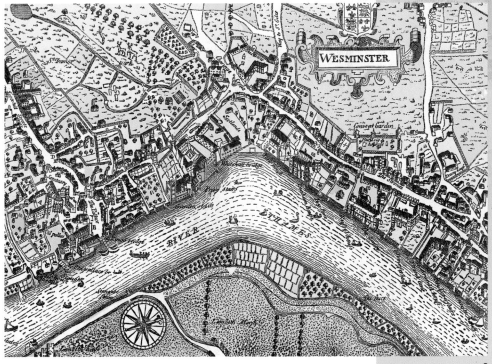

A reconstructed Saxon beehive or 'skep'

Inset: A rare Saxon brooch discovered in Floral Street during excavations of graves by AOC Archaeology in 2000. Made of copper decorated with gold plates and gold wire and set with a mosaic of polished garnets, it is thought to have possibly belonged to a woman of noble or royal birth

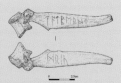

A sheep's thoracic vertebrae found near Covent Garden bearing Anglo-Saxon runic inscriptions 'T a t b e r h t' an Old English masculine name and 'd r i c' possibly 'Dagric' or 'Dairic', another masculine name. This significant find is thought to be casual carving for amusement, possibly after a meal

Recent findings take the area back to Saxon times. The Romans had abandoned the walled 'Londinium' in 410 AD and it is thought that London was mostly uninhabited for another 200 years until, as recent archaeological discoveries suggest, the Saxons created a port called Lundenwic during the 7th century.

The Saxons preferred open spaces and Lundenwic ran along the Thames to the west of the old Roman city, around the Aldwych area, along the Strand foreshore between the River Fleet (now covered by Farringdon St) and Trafalgar Square. The Venerable Bede, writing c731 AD, describes it as "a metropolis… a mart of many peoples coming by land and sea,"

Over the last 30 years, excavations in several Covent Garden sites, including the old Jubilee Hall, James St and the Lyceum Theatre, have uncovered Saxon buildings, both domestic and industrial, alongside animal remains such as cattle, sheep, pigs and fowl. The findings of various cereal grains too would indicate that the Saxons here led a fairly self-sufficient lifestyle.

Artefacts including pottery wares and quernstones used for corn grinding were found; some of these would have been imported, suggesting that the Saxons were engaged in foreign trade. Evidence of crafts such as weaving, ironworking and bone and antler working have been discovered together with the very rare finding of the remains of a colony of honeybees in James St.

This was particularly exciting as it was the earliest known bee colony to be found in an archaeological site in Britain. The bees would have been kept in hives called skeps. Honey was used not only as food but also as a medicine for antiseptic healing; the Saxons were also very fond of the alcoholic drink mead derived from the honeycomb. In addition, beeswax was produced to use as ointments and polish, much as it is today.

Tatberht lived on a farmstead near Covent Garden between the 8th and 9th centuries. He was a literate man since he elegantly inscribed his name into a sheep's bone taken from the dinner table

Saxon cremation vessels from excavations at the London Transport Museum site

Several burial sites were unearthed in the Covent Garden area containing not only human remains but various artefacts including spearheads, buckles and brooches. Alterations to the London Transport Museum unearthed evidence of Lundenwic's first cemetery; archaeologists discovered cremation vessels, human remains and jewellery dating from between AD 550 and 650, making them the first cremation burials in Lundenwic to be found and also the only burials relating to this Early Saxon period.

During work on the new wing of the Royal Opera House in 1996, the main Saxon road was unearthed beneath the car park, in addition to numerous artefacts including coins and pottery. However, this rich port was an attractive target for the Danish Vikings; the ferocity of their repeated attacks caused King Alfred the Great (b849 ruled 871-899) to re-fortify the Roman city in around 886 AD as protection for the Saxons who retreated behind these walls. Lundenwic was abandoned and became known as the 'old wic' and in turn, 'Aldwych'.

Recent excavations at the St Martin's Courtyard development site are one of the most extensive to have been undertaken within the Middle Saxon trading port of Lundenwic with the many artefacts found providing a further glimpse of life in Saxon London.

Archaeological excavation in progress at St Martin's Courtyard

Fragment of a decorated Saxon reticella glass bowl discovered at St Martin's Courtyard

Above: waste from horn and antler working, St James St

Far left: excavation of a Saxon burial from Floral Street

Left: mid 7th century skeleton of an adult male discovered in James St

Subsequently…

London's first residential square, "fit for the habitacions of Gentlemen and men of ability"

Part of the land was eventually given by the Benedictine Abbey in 1536 to King Henry VIII in exchange for some in Berkshire. When the King dissolved the monasteries in 1540 he acquired the rest of it. Edward Seymour, the Duke of Somerset was given part of the Estate in 1547 while the remaining section was granted to John Russell, the first Earl of Bedford as reward for his loyal service as a soldier and diplomat, along with many other titles and estates including those of Tavistock and Woburn.

When Seymour was beheaded for treason in 1552, John Russell received the entire estate. The Bedford family were to own the Covent Garden estate for another 400 years, becoming highly esteemed and influential with each successive monarch. Many streets in Covent Garden are named after them, including Tavistock Street and

Bedford Street. The family continue to own parts of Bloomsbury to this day. Edward Russell, the 3rd Earl, built Bedford House, a mansion, in 1586, on the north side of the Strand, where Southampton St is now. The Jubilee Hall now stands in what was part of its large garden. Sadly, nothing of this elegant mansion remains, the house being demolished in 1705-6 to make way for redevelopment.

Edward's cousin, Francis Russell, took control of the estate in 1619, becoming the 4th Earl in 1627. He was a shrewd man and an early 'property developer', quickly realising Covent Garden's potential. He paid King Charles I what was then the enormous sum of £2,000 to obtain a licence to build a number of houses to the north of his garden wall which in his words would be "fit for the habitacions of Gentlemen and men of ability."

Right: Francis, 4th Earl of Bedford

Far right: John Russell, 1st Earl of Bedford

PLAN OF BEDFORD HOUSE, COVENT GARDEN, &c. TA

From a Drawing in the Possession of

Strype's ward map of 1755, produced for Stow's survey

The Piazza
The magnificent focal point of Covent Garden

From top: Inigo Jones

Oliver Cromwell

From an engraving by Sutton Nicholls c1720

Inigo Jones, England's best known architect, had been appointed as the Surveyor of King's Works in 1613 and he was engaged to design the Italianate central square of Covent Garden, the first public square of its kind in London.

Inigo Jones was born in 1573, the son of a Smithfield cloth worker. He served an apprenticeship as a joiner but was so talented that he was fortunate enough to study the works of such great designers as Vencenzo Scamozzi and Andrea Palladio in Italy. His huge admiration for their classical style influenced his own architectural designs, including those of the Queen's House at Greenwich and the Banqueting House in Whitehall.

The square featured St. Paul's Church to the west side and grand terraced houses on the north and east sides which looked inwards over the large open courtyard. To the south, the Piazza bordered the wall at the back of the Bedford House garden. Unfortunately, none of the original splendid houses remain but they were four storeys high with colonnaded front doors; they had gardens and coach houses with stabling at the back, certainly houses fit for the gentry. Many early residents were titled noblemen such as Sir William Alexander, first Earl of Stirling and Sir Thomas Wentworth, first Earl of Strafford.

However, the elegance suffered a slow decline with the coming of the Civil War in 1642. Oliver Cromwell, leader of the Parliamentarians and later to become the Lord Protector of the Realm, came to live in nearby Drury Lane along with other Parliamentarians. Many of the Royalist residents were forced to flee. After the Restoration of Charles II in 1660, some of the Royalist sympathisers drifted back but many of the rich aristocratic families now preferred the more fashionable developments of Mayfair and St. James's. This left some of the fine houses surrounding the Piazza empty and open to vandalism; the Piazza began to deteriorate. Covent Garden became a centre of entertainment; it was taken over by many theatres, taverns, coffee houses, brothels and gaming rooms whose patrons included writers, musicians, actors and playboys seeking pleasure.

The Piazza and its surrounding streets are always full of mime artists, buskers, jugglers and other street entertainers. Covent Garden is still a place full of fun and entertainment!

The Great Plague

The outbreak of bubonic plague, a disease carried by the fleas that infested the black rat, was especially severe in London

The first known victim was Margaret Ponteous, who died in Covent Garden in April 1665, as shown by the Bills of Mortality drawn up at the time to record the death rate.

100,000 Londoners were dead by November of that year. Samuel Pepys wrote in his famous diary, "this day, much against my will, I did in Drury Lane see two or three houses marked with a red cross upon the doors", the crosses indicating that the inhabitants had become sick with the disease.

Plague doctors wore beak-like masks which were filled with aromatic herbs and spices to protect them from the foul air which was believed to carry the plague. There was no cure; the bodies had to be carried away at night in carts, the drivers ringing handbells, calling "Bring out your dead!" before taking them to be buried in mass pits in the fields beyond the suburbs. 15,239 people perished in Covent Garden alone. The plague was eventually halted by the Great Fire of London in 1666, which stopped just short of Covent Garden.

Above: not real doctors at all; a recreation of a plague doctor's dress by Scottish artist Frank To

Urban legend has it that the symptoms of the plague gave rise to the children's nursery rhyme:
**'Ring a ring o' roses
A pocket full of posies
A-tishoo, a-tishoo,
We all fall down.'**

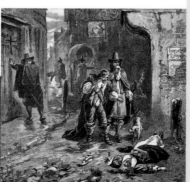

The Great Plague Of London which killed around a fifth of the city's population. From Cassell's Illustrated History of England, 1865

Market porters and below, flower sellers from 'Street Life in London', by journalists J. Thomson and Adolphe Smith, 1877

Covent Garden became the largest wholesale fruit and vegetable market in England but it began humbly in the 1600s with a few market stalls and benches under the trees by the Bedford House garden wall. The market sold fruit, vegetables, flowers and herbs. In 1670 Charles II granted the fifth Earl of Bedford and his heirs the right to hold a market every day of the year except Sunday and Christmas, for the buying and selling of 'fruit, flowers, roots and herbs'.

During the 18th century, goods such as caged birds, alcohol and baked items appeared in addition to those fruit and vegetables allowed by the original Royal Charter and the market became noisy and messy.

The fine buildings in the square were abandoned by the gentry in favour of the more fashionable areas of Bloomsbury and Mayfair; the houses were turned into seedy lodging houses, brothels and taverns. The first brothel or 'bagnio' was opened in 1681 by Robert Lazenby and others soon followed, along with Turkish baths called Hummums. The Hummums Hotel is mentioned in Charles Dickens's 'Great Expectations'; the London Transport Museum and Tutton's Brasserie now cover the site.

The early 1800s saw the market expanding and becoming more congested. The alleys around it had been taken over by manufacturers including tailors, barrow-makers and goldsmiths.

Bedford Chambers, 9, The Piazza, is a Grade II listed building

The 1860 Floral Hall designed by E.M. Barry

A new market building was designed by Charles Fowler in 1833, looking much the same as it does today, with its perimeter colonnade and lodges, but without roofs which were added later. It housed fruiterers and plant and cut-flower sellers. Other market buildings followed; the Floral Hall, designed by E.M. Barry in 1860 had an arched glass roof and dome (sadly destroyed by a fire in 1956) and was intended as a flower market but in fact was used for foreign fruit trade. A permanent flower market was built for the flower sellers in 1870 on the south-east corner of the Piazza; these buildings are now occupied by The London Transport Museum and until January 2007, the Theatre Museum. Some parts of the portico from the Floral Hall have been used in the transformation of Southwark's Borough Market near London Bridge. In 1904 the Jubilee Market was built by Cubitt and Howard for the sale of cut flowers.

The market was a colourful, lively place but totally disorganised and chaotic! The Bedford family decided to sell it in 1918 to The Covent Garden Estate Company Ltd owned by the Beecham family, of medical renown. It became an institution! Each working day began at midnight; porters arrived in trains and buses to unload lorry loads of crates containing roses, lettuces, cabbages, potatoes, apples and other produce from Britain's market gardens.

Covent Garden Market, Balthazar Nebot 1730-1762

Covent Garden Strawberry Seller from the series 'Cries of London', 1804

Inset: Market porters, early 1900s

The porters carried the crates on their heads or in barrows, to the stalls. Here, the 'nightmen' set up the displays, opening around 400 boxes each. The displays had to be ready by 4.30 am for the arrival of the buyers at 5 am. The market was all over by 11 am but still the hustle and bustle continued with lorries dropping off next day supplies and re-loading for deliveries. The market was eventually sold to the Covent Garden Market Authority in 1961 and moved to Nine Elms in 1974.

The original Covent Garden market site was restored by the Greater London Council; the central market has been converted into many small shops and eating places, with colourful stalls selling arts and crafts and the Jubilee

Hall is now a covered street market.

Upon the abolition of the GLC in 1985, the Covent Garden Area Trust was formed to maintain control over development, thereby safeguarding and conserving the area's heritage; it was granted particular powers over its 'Protected Lands' ie the Central Market, 25-31 James St, 10 Floral St, Bedford Chambers, Cubitts Yard and the Museum Block.

The Apple Market at Christmas

The London Transport Museum

London's transport network is used by millions of people and the Museum brings to life the development of this system.

Exciting displays chart the birth of the buses, trains and trams which make up London's transport network; for instance, visitors can learn how the growth of London led to the world's first Underground railway originally served by steam engines and view an original underground train from 1863 which is on display.

The Museum also houses a world-class collection of graphic art, including colourful pioneering travel advertising posters and artwork.

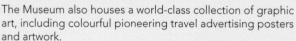

The portico, St Paul's

Niche containing the actress Ellen Terry's ashes

St. Paul's Church, designed by Inigo Jones, is all that is left of the original 17th century development. Supposedly it was the first location of the Eleanor Cross (the replica is now located in the front of Charing Cross Station) and it is the site where all distances to London are officially measured. St Paul's was the first new Anglican church to be built in London following the Reformation.

According to the 18th century gossip, Horace Walpole, Jones was told by the 4th Earl of Bedford to keep the costs low, saying "in short, I would not have it much better than a barn." To which, Jones replied "Well then, you shall have the handsomest barn in England."

It was Jones's intention that the main entrance should be at the east end of the building opening onto the Piazza but the Bishop of London, William Laud, insisted that tradition should be followed with the altar placed against the east wall; the door could not therefore be used. Side doors were used instead, with the main entrance at the west door opening onto a small churchyard and country lane (which later became Bedford Street). The church is oblong in shape with tall, arched windows and has a simple interior.

A major restoration was undertaken in 1788 by the architect Thomas Hardwick, which included facing the interior with Portland stone. However a huge blaze in 1795, caused by builders leaving their fire unguarded during their lunch break, destroyed nearly all the work that had been done. Hardwick rebuilt the church, reproducing Inigo Jones's design faithfully. The pulpit, said to be the work of Grinling Gibbons, the artist and woodcarver, or one of his pupils, was saved, along with the parish records. The organ was made in 1861

> **Well then, you shall have the handsomest barn in England**

A limewood wreath by Grinling Gibbons, presented by the Dean and Chapter of St Pauls Cathedral.

The simple interior of St Paul's

by Henry Bevington, using part of the case designed by Hardwick in 1795.

The church has many famous associations; John Wesley preached here and the artist J.M.W. Turner was baptized here in 1775, as was the dramatist W.S. Gilbert in 1837. Grinling Gibbons was buried in the churchyard in 1721, as well as the artist Peter Lely in 1680, the composer Thomas Arne (he composed 'Rule Britannia') in 1778, and the actor Charles Macklin in 1792, amongst notable others. The actress Ellen Terry died in 1928 and her ashes are kept in a casket on the south wall.

Because of its long association with the theatre, the church is known as 'the Actors' Church'. Memorial services for members of the theatrical profession are held here and there are numerous wall plaques commemorating famous personalities including Noel Coward, Ivor Novello, Charlie Chaplin and Vivien Leigh.

The portico provides the opening scene for George Bernard Shaw's play 'Pygmalion' in which Professor Higgins meets the flower girl Eliza Doolittle. The play was made into the musical 'My Fair Lady' following Shaw's death and in 1964 Audrey Hepburn starred in the award winning film by Warner Bros.

It was also here that supposedly the first ever Punch and Judy show was staged, witnessed and recorded by Samuel Pepys, as shown by an inscription on the wall, dated 1662. A yearly festival of puppetry is still hosted here every May.

Building work began in 1631 on the west side of the Piazza and was completed in 1633, at a cost of £4,400, although it was not consecrated until 1638. Covent Garden became a separate parish in 1645.

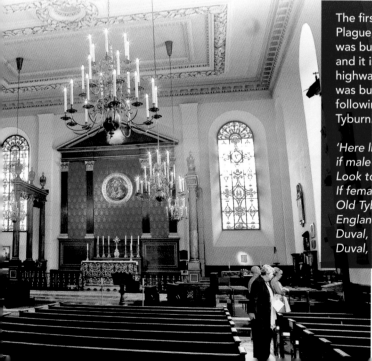

The first victim of the Great Plague, Margaret Ponteous, was buried here in 1665, and it is thought that the highwayman Claude Duval was buried here in 1670 following his execution at Tyburn. His epitaph reads:

'Here lies Duval, Reader, if male thou art, Look to thy purse. If female, to thy heart. Old Tyburn's glory, England's illustrious Thief, Duval, the ladies' joy; Duval, the gentleman's grief.'

St. Clement Danes

"Oranges and lemons" say the bells of St Clement's

The nave of the church looking towards the altar. The Royal Coat of Arms is located on the ceiling

Aerial shot of Aldwych with St Clement Danes surrounded by trees

Built on an island where the Strand meets Aldwych, St Clement Danes is today the central church of the Royal Air Force but it is thought to have originated as a small wooden building before the 11th century. A stone church followed, in the reign of the Danish king, Canute, dedicated to St. Clement, the patron saint of sailors; this is symbolised by an anchor on the church's nameplate. Later, the church was in the care of the Knights Templar for almost 150 years, from 1170-1312.

Sir Christopher Wren designed a new building in 1680-82, incorporating what was left of the old stone tower. James Gibbs, added an elegant steeple in 1719 and Grinling Gibbons, the woodcarver, has been credited with the pulpit inside.

Eight bells were cast in the Whitechapel Foundry with two more added in 1844. They were made famous by the nursery rhyme 'oranges and lemons' and suffered serious damage in the Blitz of World War II; only the Sanctus bell, cast in 1588, survived, the others having to be recast in 1956. The 'oranges and lemons' chimes were introduced in 1920 and the bells peal out the tune five times per day.

Famous parishioners include the writer Dr. Samuel Johnson, the poet John Donne and the actor David Garrick. One of the conspirators in the Gunpowder Plot of 1605, Thomas Winter, gave evidence that the plans to assassinate King James I of England and VI of Scotland had been devised behind this church. Ironically perhaps, the man who thwarted these schemes, Robert Cecil, Earl of Salisbury, had been baptised here.

It is thought that the game of rugby football was created through the antics of the rector of 1843-1855, William Webb-Ellis. Whilst a pupil at Rugby School, he ignored the rules of football by running with the ball in his arms. A snuff box belonging to him is displayed to the right of the main entrance.

During World War II the church was badly bomb damaged but the original Grinling Gibbons pulpit survives because it had been taken to St. Paul's Cathedral to be kept safe. The church was restored in 1955-8 using donations from the RAF and Commonwealth and Allied Air Forces.

There are several hundred hand-carved slate RAF squadron badges set into the floor and the Books of Remembrance hold the names of 150,000 RAF men and women killed in service. Underneath the west gallery is a book containing the names of 1,900 American airmen, based in Britain, who lost their lives in the Second World War. The organ, designed by Ralph Downes, was a gift from the United States Air Force.

"Oranges and lemons" say the bells of St. Clement's,
"You owe me five farthings" say the bells of St. Martin's,
"When will you pay me?" ask the bells of Old Bailey,
"When I grow rich," say the bells of Shoreditch,
"When will that be?" ask the bells of Stepney ("Step-knee")
"I do not know," say the great bells of Bow.
Here comes a candle to light you to bed,
Here comes a chopper to chop off your head,
Chip - chop, chip - chop, the last - man's - dead.

Outside, in front of the church, is a statue of Arthur 'Bomber' Harris, (1892-1984) which was erected in 1992. Bomber Harris was Commander in Chief of Bomber Command and Air Chief Marshal in World War II and he oversaw the bombing of many German cities including Dresden. Although his methods were criticised because of the number of civilian casualties, he believed that massive and sustained area bombing would hasten Germany's surrender. The statue was unveiled by Queen Elizabeth, the Queen Mother in 1992, amid controversy in both Germany and Britain.

Above: Arthur 'Bomber' Harris, Commander in Chief of Bomber Command and Air Chief Marshal in World War II

St Giles, designed in the Palladian style

The church in St. Giles High St, is dedicated to the patron saint of outcasts and lepers and was founded as a leper hospital in 1101 by Matilda, wife of Henry I. The present building was designed and built by Henry Flitcroft, the son of William III's gardener, and opened on Christmas Day 1733.

Its 75 volumes of parish registers date back to 1561 and contain many famous names. Burials include George Chapman who translated Homer in 1634, with a memorial in the church said to have been designed by Inigo Jones, Andrew Marvell, the poet in 1678, the artist Sir Godfrey Kneller in 1723 and, although his body was later exhumed, the Archbishop of Armagh, Oliver Plunkett, was buried here in 1681 having been hanged, drawn and quartered at Tyburn for treason. He was the last Roman Catholic martyred in England and canonised in 1975. There is a tombstone to Richard Penderell, a woodman who helped to hide Charles II in the 'royal oak' of Boscobel after the Battle of Worcester in 1651.

The poet John Milton's daughter Mary was baptised in 1694 whilst Lord Byron's daughter Allegra and two of Shelley's children were baptised together in 1818.

The actor David Garrick was married here in 1749 as was the actress Frances Kemble in 1786; fellow actress Mrs Siddons's signature can be seen as a witness.

St. Giles Church is notable for the giving of the

St Giles in the Fields. Major restoration work in the 1950s was described by John Betjeman as 'one of the most successful postwar church restorations'

The Resurrection.
An intricate carving from the 17th century gate based on Michelangelo's painting of the resurrection in the Sistine Chapel

'St Giles Bowl', a last mug of ale given to prisoners on their way to execution at Tyburn. These prisoners were later buried in the St Giles churchyard. It was here also, in the parish of St Giles, that the Great Plague first began in 1665. There were 3,216 deaths in the parish, with 1,361 in one month alone; the church suffered structural damage caused by the sheer number of burials.

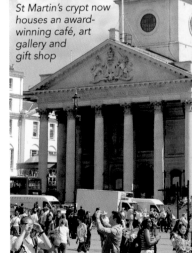

St Martin's crypt now houses an award-winning café, art gallery and gift shop

St. Mary le Strand
The 'Wrens' church dominates The Strand

In 1711 an Act was passed by Parliament to build 50 new churches in London and St. Mary le Strand was the first of these 'Queen Anne Churches' to be built. The original church had been demolished in 1549 to make way for Edward, Duke of Somerset's new palace, the first Somerset House.

Designed by James Gibbs, the present church was completed in 1724 in an Italianate style, one of the loveliest of its kind in England. The church contains many fine carvings and ornate decorations, such as a beautifully embellished ceiling.

Charles Edward Stuart, or Bonnie Prince Charlie as he is better known, is thought to have made a secret visit here in 1750 and Charles Dickens's parents were married in the church in 1809. It has been the official church of the Women's Royal Naval Service (the Wrens) since 1984 and the outside features in the opening sequence of the film *Chariots of Fire*.

The ornate ceiling by John and Chrysostom Wilkins and richly decorated apse dominate the inside of the church. The ten nave windows have been re-glazed using glass made in the style of the 18th century

St. Martin-in-the-Fields
The parish church of Buckingham Palace

The present church, situated at the north-east corner of Trafalgar Square, was another designed and built by James Gibbs in 1726, but records show a church on this site as early as the thirteenth century.

The church was designed with a grand Corinthian portico comprising of six columns raised on a flight of steps; this gives the impression that the steeple sits on the roof whereas it actually stands behind the portico. Inside, there are special pews at Gallery level - one a royal pew to the left of the altar and the other an Admiralty pew. It is the parish church of Buckingham Palace and St. James's Palace and there have

been several royal christenings here including that of Charles II in 1630. Burials here include the craftsman Thomas Chippendale, the artist Joshua Reynolds, Jack Sheppard the highwayman and Nell Gwynne, the mistress of Charles II.

The church's crypt served as a shelter for homeless soldiers and others during World War I and as an air raid shelter in WWII. Today, it accommodates a gift shop, the London Brass Rubbing Centre, award-winning *Café in the Crypt* and is also a well known classical concert venue. Nearby, the charity *The Connection at St Martin-in-the-Fields* provides support for the homeless.

Installed in 2008, St Martin's east window is the work of artist Shirazeh Houshiary and depicts a cross as if reflected in water

This is London's oldest theatre, originally built in 1663 for Thomas Killigrew under one of two patents granted by Charles II; the other patent was granted to the Covent Garden Theatre, now the Royal Opera House. It was here that Charles II met his mistress Nell Gwynne; she famously sold oranges at the theatre as a child and made her acting debut here in 1665.

The present building is actually the fourth to be built; the first was destroyed by fire in 1672 and a second was opened in 1674. Sarah Siddons, Charles Kemble and Charles Macklin were among many actors to perform here. The famous actor David Garrick was the manager from 1747 to 1776, during which time the theatre enjoyed success with its Shakespearian productions. The playwright Richard Brinsley Sheridan took over the management and his play *The School for Scandal* was first performed here in 1777.
This second building was thought

unsafe and demolished with its replacement opening in 1794. Despite possessing the world's first safety curtain, it burnt down in 1809. Sheridan, who still owned the patent, stood watching the blazing building, drinking a glass of port and declared, "surely a gentleman can have a drink by his own fireside"! The present building opened in 1812. Augustus Harris became manager in 1879 when the theatre became famous for its melodramatic shows with spectacular stage effects portraying earthquakes, avalanches and the like. Pantomimes were performed each Christmas and many fine performers trod the boards

*From top: Charles II. Detail from **The Meeting** by Rita Greer*

David Garrick

Charles Macklin

Inset: Sarah Siddons

Right: Scene from 'Anthony and Cleopatra' at the Drury Lane Theatre in 1873

here, including Edmund Kean, Dan Leno and the great clown Joseph Grimaldi.

During the 1900s the theatre became known for musicals; *Rose Marie*, *The Desert Song* and *Show Boat* were produced in the 1920s whilst the theatre put on Ivor Novello operettas including *Glamorous Night* and *Crest of the Wave* in the '30s.

The theatre was the headquarters of the Entertainment National Service Association (Ensa- or more popularly translated as *Every Night Something Awful*) during World War II and post-war, many more favourite musicals were produced, notably those of Rodgers and Hammerstein, including *Oklahoma!*, *Carousel*, *South Pacific* and *The King and I*. The theatre staged the long-running *My Fair Lady* in the 1950s and *Camelot* and *Hello, Dolly!*

in the '60s, with Cameron Mackintosh's *Miss Saigon* playing for ten years at the theatre from 1989. Many great performers have entertained the public here during this time; the likes of Anna Neagle, Paul Robeson, Ivor Novello, Howard Keel, Mary Martin, Julie Andrews, Ginger Rogers and Michael Crawford, to name but a few.

The theatre displays a copy of the original Royal Charter which is still in operation today and every monarch since the Restoration has visited; indeed, the theatre boasts two royal boxes. There have been more than one assassination attempts on its royal patrons - in 1716 a man named Freeman tried to shoot George II, and then in 1800 there was an attempt on the life of his grandson, George III.

Nell Gwynne

Inset: A poster from the era of Augustus Harris

Below left: The auditorium

Below: The Augustus Harris memorial drinking fountain. Decorated with masonic symbols in recognition of his membership, both the building and the memorial are Grade I listed

The Royal Opera House
Home to The Royal Ballet and the Royal Opera Companies

Tour group, front of house

The first Theatre Royal, Covent Garden, as it was then known, was built in 1728 by the actor/manager John Rich, a celebrated harlequin and pantomimist, using money obtained from his commission of *The Beggar's Opera*.

The theatre opened in 1732 with a performance of Congreve's *The Way of the World*; William Hogarth engraved Rich's triumphant arrival when he was carried in by his actors.

For around a hundred years, the theatre staged mainly plays; however Rich developed the art of pantomime and these became a Covent Garden tradition until the late 1930s.

Many of Handel's operas and oratorios were first performed here and his theatre organ was left to John Rich upon his death in 1759. Unfortunately a fire in 1808 destroyed the building along with many valuable contents including the organ and Handel's manuscripts; a spark from an actor's gun was thought to be the cause and such

was the blaze that twenty-three firemen perished.

The 'Sublime Society of Beef Steaks', a club founded by John Rich which met for a beef-steak dinner in the theatre every Saturday from November to June, lost all its wine and had to relocate to the Bedford Coffee House (1808-09).

A second theatre building opened in 1809. The management which included the famous sister and brother actors, John Philip Kemble and Sarah Siddons, raised the ticket prices to recover the cost of rebuilding; this sparked off the 'Old Price Riots' on the first night, with the audience hissing, booing and beating sticks. The magistrates were called in to read 'the Riot Act' but the riots continued for over two months until the old prices were reinstated.

The theatre became the Royal Italian Opera in 1847 and opened with a performance of Rossini's *Semiramide*. However, fire again destroyed the theatre in 1856. A third building was designed by E.M. Barry in a classical Italian style; Barry also designed the Floral Hall next door which was re-named the Paul Hamlyn Hall in 2007 in appreciation of financial aid given by the publisher.

This third building had disastrous beginnings - one of the construction workers fell to his death whilst admiring some of the stonework and on the opening night, the final act of the long opera *Les Huguenots* had to be cancelled because the audience had taken too long to reach their seats at the start!

Augustus Harris became manager in 1888, installing electric lighting and employing well-loved singers; the theatre enjoyed great success and was re-named the Royal Opera House in 1892. Many first performances were given here, including Wagner's *The Ring* conducted by Gustav Mahler.

The theatre was used as a furniture store during World War I and as a dance hall in the Second World War. Boosey and Hawkes, the music publishers acquired the lease in 1945, opening the theatre again in 1946 as the national Opera House.

Jullien's Bal Masque, Covent Garden Theatre, c1847

The Sadlers Wells Ballet became the resident ballet company, under Ninette de Valois, and the opening night saw Margot Fonteyn dancing as Aurora in *The Sleeping Beauty*. A new opera company was formed, the Covent Garden Opera Company. Both companies went on to receive Royal Charters, becoming the Royal Ballet in 1956 and the Royal Opera in 1968.

Many great names have performed at the Royal Opera House, as it became known, including Margot Fonteyn, Moira Shearer and Robert Helpmann in extravagant ballet productions, and Joan Sutherland and Kiri Te Kanawa among many great singers.

Backstage at the Royal Opera House

Major development began in 1997 with a new wing along Russell St. designed by Dixon Jones. The Royal Opera House was reopened in 1999 boasting wonderful modern facilities - bright new dressing rooms, rehearsal studios and a state-of-the-art theatre. The Floral Hall was completely renovated, creating a spectacular public area of eating places and bars.

A tour in progress

The Royal Ballet has its permanent home here, together with the Royal Opera and the Orchestra of the Royal Opera House, providing the highest quality venue for opera and ballet lovers alike. Backstage or auditorium tours provide a valuable insight into the history and redevelopment of the theatre and behind-the-scenes technology. You may even get to see the Royal Ballet in class!

The Lyceum - Wellington Street
The first London theatre to be lit by gas

In the 1960s
and '70s,
the Lyceum
hosted
concerts from
such stars as
The Who,
Bob Marley,
Culture Club
and Iggy Pop

The first theatre of this name was built in 1765 on a nearby site, as a room for concerts and exhibitions. It was used at various times as a circus, a chapel and a concert room; in 1802, Madame Tussaud used it for her first waxworks exhibition in London.

Performances were given by the Drury Lane Company following the Theatre Royal fire and it was here that the 'Sublime Society of Beef Steaks', founded by Henry Rich, held their meetings from 1809-1830; the members, never more than twenty-four in number, met every Saturday night to eat beef steaks and drink port wine.

The theatre became famous as the first in London to be lit by gas and for staging the London premiere of Mozart's opera *Cosi Fan Tutti*.

The Lyceum was rebuilt in 1815 to a design by Samuel Beazley. This however burnt down in 1830, to be replaced by a second Beazley design on the present site in 1834; it was the first theatre in England to have a balcony overhanging the circle.

The accomplished actor, Henry Irving, took over the management in 1878, employing Ellen Terry as his leading lady and the theatre was to enjoy a very successful time, staging many Shakespearian productions including *Hamlet* and *The Merchant of Venice*. Bram Stoker was business manager from 1878 – 1898; his 1897 novel *Dracula* used Henry Irving and his dramatic mannerisms as the inspiration for the character of Count Dracula.

1904 saw the Lyceum rebuilt again by Bertie Crewe, preserving the original Beazley façade and portico. It opened as a music and variety hall but went on to present dramas and from 1951 became the Lyceum Ballroom for a long period of time. It is said that the afternoon sessions were legendary as a place for young men to pick up girls! Mecca also pioneered bingo in the dancehall. In the 1960s and '70s, it hosted many concerts and performances from such stars as The Who, Bob Marley, Culture Club and Iggy Pop.

The theatre was restored in 1996, opening with Andrew Lloyd Webber's *Jesus Christ Superstar*. Since 1999, it has staged the hugely popular Disney musical *The Lion King*.

The Lyceum Theatre

The New London Theatre, Drury Lane

The present theatre is a modern building but the site has been a centre of entertainment since Elizabethan times. There have been several buildings with various names including 'the Middlesex Music Hall' in 1851 and 'the New Middlesex Theatre of Varieties' in 1911, going on to become 'the Winter Gardens Theatre' in 1919.

Many musical productions and plays were staged until 1959 when the theatre was sold to a property developer. The site stood idle for a length of time but the theatre re-opened in a new building, designed by Paul Tvrtkovic and Sean Kenny, in 1973, as the New London Theatre.

The Andrew Lloyd Webber musical *Cats* had its debut here in 1981 and became one of the longest running musicals in West End and Broadway history, with its final performance in 2002. More recently, the theatre has been the home of *War Horse*, a play using life-sized puppets based on the acclaimed novel by Michael Morpurgo.

The Duchess Theatre, Catherine Street

Opening in 1929, the theatre is one of the smallest in London. Many notable and popular productions have been staged here, including T.S.Eliot's *Murder in the Cathedral* in 1939 and *Oh, Calcutta* in 1974. Noel Coward's *Blithe Spirit* and Pinter's *The Caretaker* also had successful runs.

The Fortune Theatre, Russell Street

Standing on the site of an old tavern, the theatre opened in 1924 and was the first to be built in London after World War I. It was designed by Ernest Schaufelberg who sculpted the bronze "Nude Girl' on the façade.

Many distinguished actors and actresses such as Dame Judi Dench and Dirk Bogarde have performed here. Successful productions include Flanders and Swann in *At the Drop of a Hat* in 1957 and *Beyond the Fringe* with the original line-up of Peter Cook and Dudley Moore, Jonathan Miller and Alan Bennett. The theatre has most recently become associated with the long running production of *The Woman in Black*, a ghostly drama adapted by Stephen Mallatratt from the novel by Susan Hill.

The New London Theatre

The Fortune Theatre

Inset: Ernest Schaufelberg's Nude Girl

The Duchess Theatre

The Adelphi Theatre - The Strand
Said to be haunted by William Terriss

The original theatre was built in 1806 by John Scott, a local tradesman, and was called *The Sans Pareil* changing to *Adelphi* in 1819. The present building is the fourth on the site, opening in December 1930.

Various popular entertainment productions have been staged here, melodramas and opera, Shakespearian plays and dance, but it is now best known and loved for modern musicals including the hugely popular and long running revivals of *Me and My Girl* and *Chicago* which both ran for over eight years.

It was outside the stage door that a leading actor of the time, William Terriss, was savagely stabbed and killed on 16th December 1897. His murderer was a supporting actor called Richard Prince who was madly jealous of Terriss; judged to be insane, he ended his days in Broadmoor Prison. Terriss died inside the theatre in the arms of Jessie Milward, his leading lady and mistress. It is said that his last words were "I will be back".

The façade of the Adelphi Theatre from a hand-coloured engraving of 1840

The Garrick Theatre, Charing Cross Road

The theatre, designed by Walter Emden, opened in April 1889, with seating for 800 people. Strangely, it is said that one of the resident cats was named as a shareholder in this theatre!

The beautiful gold leaf auditorium was restored in 1986 by designer Carl Toms and the top gallery has been closed, reducing seating capacity to 656.

The Garrick is mostly associated with comedy and comedy-drama productions including *An Inspector Calls* and *No Sex Please, We're British*.

Right:
Charing Cross Road and the Garrick Theatre in 1902. From a sepia-tinted postcard

The Donmar Warehouse, Earlham St

Fringe theatre has sprung up in some of the warehouses following the closure of the Covent Garden Market. The most notable of these, the Donmar Warehouse, is a small not-for-profit theatre with seating for only 251 people.

The Donmar company was formed in 1953 by the producer Donald Albery who formed the name by taking the first three letters of both his name and those of his friend, the prima ballerina Margot Fonteyn. He bought the site which had been a vat room and hops warehouse, in 1961. It was adapted as a private drama studio and rehearsal room for the London Festival Ballet.

The Royal Shakespeare Company acquired it in 1977, renaming it *The Warehouse* and staging many acclaimed productions. In 1990 the theatre was bought and rebuilt by Roger Wingate who gave it its present name. Sam Mendes was appointed as Artistic Director in 1992 and during the ten years of his direction, the theatre became one of the most exciting venues in London. Michael Grandage succeeded Mendes in 2002 and to this day, the Donmar Warehouse is acclaimed for producing new plays, revamping old classics and putting on small-scale musicals. Many well-known actors have appeared at the theatre, including Nicole Kidman, Gwyneth Paltrow, Ian McKellen, Ewan McGregor, Kenneth Branagh and Dame Judi Dench. Josie Rourke followed on from Grandage as the new Artistic Director from January 2012.

In February 2011, the Donmar, together with the National Theatre Live programme, broadcast its production of *King Lear* with Derek Jacobi in the title role, to cinemas in 20 countries around the world. With 350 screens, it meant that the single performance was seen by more than 40,000 people.

The Donmar Warehouse

Coffee, said to taste like 'syrup of soot and essence of old shoes' was seen to 'prevent drowsiness'

Coffee houses appeared in London during the latter half of the 17th century and were soon established as places where people from all walks of life could meet and relax, drinking coffee, smoking, writing and discussing ideas and topics of the day. Lloyd's of London owes its name to the coffee house in the City of London where the insurance underwriters conducted their business around 1700. The Royal Society of Arts was established in 1754 in Rawthmell's Coffee House, Covent Garden.

Previously, men had exchanged ideas and carried out business in the taverns but these were often rowdy, chaotic places where the ale consumed rendered business largely unproductive. Coffee, said to taste like 'syrup of soot and essence of old shoes' was seen to 'prevent drowsiness and make one fit for business'. The coffee houses had a huge impact on political, literary and social life; writers, diarists, merchants, professionals and other intellectuals met in them, including Samuel Pepys, Samuel Johnson and Joshua Reynolds.

Not everyone approved of the coffee houses or 'penny universities' as they were known but they were approved by the church since they did not serve alcohol. Women, who were banned from them, took exception to the time their husbands spent therein, launching the 'Women's Petition Against Coffee' in 1674. King Charles II tried unsuccessfully to ban them as being places where men became seditious, spreading rumours about the King and his government. Several were established in Covent Garden and three of the most famous, *Will's*, *Button's* and *Tom's* stood on Russell Street.

Will's - on the corner of Russell Street and Bow Street. William Urwin established this venue which was known as 'the Wits' coffee house. Here, the patrons held serious discussions of literature whilst sipping their coffee. John Dryden the poet was such a regular customer here that he had a chair reserved by the fire for him in winter and another on a balcony overlooking Bow Street for the summer. Other visitors included the poet Alexander Pope and Samuel Pepys who enjoyed "witty and pleasant discourse" here.

Tom's - on the first floor of number 17 Russell Street. It was established in 1700 by Thomas West, who threw himself to his death from a second-floor window in 1722 whilst suffering an extreme attack of gout. Here, noblemen mixed with commoners and, as Mackey says in his *Journey through England*, they enjoyed "the universal liberty of Speech of the English nation". Frequent visitors included Dr. Samuel Johnson, the actor David Garrick, the artist Sir Joshua Reynolds and the dramatist Oliver Goldsmith.

Tom's became a private club in 1768 where, for an annual fee, members had the use of a card room and other facilities.

An historically accurate representation
of a typical 17c Coffee House

Patron of *Old Slaughter's Coffee House*, William Hogarth established The *St Martin's Lane Academy* in 1735, later to become *The Royal Academy*. The *Society for the Prevention of Cruelty to Animals* (to receive royal patronage in 1840 becoming the *RSPCA*) was founded here in 1824

Button's - at number 10 Russell Street

This coffee house was founded by Daniel Button in 1712. Button was a former servant of the Countess of Warwick and was set up in business by her second husband, the essayist Joseph Addison, who co-founded *The Tatler* and *The Spectator* with Sir Richard Steele. The coffee house was used as an unofficial publishing headquarters. Other famous people to frequent Button's were the writer Daniel Defoe, the poet Alexander Pope and the satirist, Jonathan Swift.

As a means of tempting the 'wits' away from Will's, Addison erected in Button's, a letter-box designed in the shape of an antique Egyptian lion; letters could be posted through the lion's jaws providing subjects for discussion and debate which could then be used in Addison's newspapers. Thus, the coffee house became the new centre of London literary life. When Button's closed in around 1731, the lion's head was moved to the Shakespeare Tavern and eventually, was taken by the Duke of Bedford to his home at Woburn Abbey.

Bedford Coffee House

This coffee house stood under the Piazza near the Covent Garden Theatre and is first chronicled in 1730. It was a favourite haunt of the actor David Garrick, the novelists John and Henry Fielding and William Hogarth the artist; Alexander Pope and Sheridan were also regular customers.

During the early 1800s, the coffee house served as a meeting place for the 'Sublime Society of Beef-Steaks',

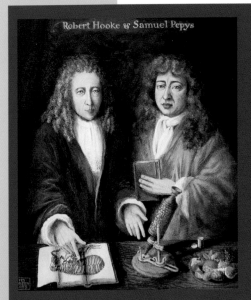

Robert Hooke (1635-1703) pictured on the left with Samuel Pepys.
An ingenious man, he was a scientist, architect and surveyor for the City of London. Made Curator of Experiments for the Royal Society, he assisted Christopher Wren in designing the Monument near London Bridge which commemorates the Great Fire of London. Hooke invented the universal joint, the iris diaphragm (as used in camera lenses) and was great friends with both Sir Christopher Wren and Samuel Pepys. A great frequenter of Coffee Houses, he is known to have set up scientific experiments (some even involving exploding glass balls) in order to have witnesses to the results. Naturally this tended to draw quite a crowd and so it was greatly encouraged by the owners!

alternating between here and the Lyceum theatre. This club, established by the theatre manager and performer John Rich in 1735, became celebrated by members who included royalty, for its weekly meetings where steaks were served accompanied by baked potatoes and copious quantities of port. Members, whose number was limited to twenty-four, were required to wear a uniform consisting of a blue coat and buff waistcoat with brass buttons bearing the words 'Beef and Liberty'. The club met at various venues till 1867 when it was disbanded briefly; however, a new club was set up in1876 which still meets in Irving Street, near Leicester Square. It was here on 7th April 1779 that the Reverend James Hackman, approached one of the theatre-goers at the end of the Covent Garden Theatre performance and shot her in the head. She, Martha Ray, a singer and mistress of the Cabinet minister Lord Sandwich had been the subject of years of his unrequited love. He then tried to shoot himself unsuccessfully and was later tried for murder and hanged at Tyburn.

Tom King's Coffee House

Was founded in the 1720s in one of the wooden buildings in Covent Garden square and became notorious as a place for upper class young men to meet prostitutes. Its owner, Tom King, had attended Eton College as a boy and had married a local girl, Moll. Apparently, they didn't have any beds in the place apart from their own, in order that they couldn't be charged with brothel-keeping! When Tom died in 1737, Moll carried on alone but was constantly up before the King's Bench for keeping a disorderly house. She died in 1747. Little is known of the house's subsequent history.

Newspapers, periodicals and the postal service can all trace their beginnings to the coffee houses of the 17th & 18th century

The Lamb and Flag

Originally built in 1623, The Lamb and Flag in Rose Street is one of the oldest surviving wooden-framed buildings in London. It is recorded as being a public house as early as 1772 when it was called The Cooper's Arms. Once known as The Bucket of Blood because of its associations with bare-knuckle fist fighting it received it's present name in 1833. The Rose Street area had a particularly bad reputation both for its prostitution and its unsanitary, sordid conditions, and it was here in 1679, that the poet John Dryden was attacked by three men. It is thought he was beaten in revenge for writing insulting verses about the Duchess of Portsmouth, Charles II's mistress. The prompt action of the landlord saved him from more serious injury. The incident is referred to on the painted board on the ceiling of the passageway beside the Lamb and Flag.

The Rose Tavern

This stood next to the Drury Lane Theatre in Russell Street and was popular with theatre-goers including Samuel Pepys. Towards the end of the 17th century the tavern had earned a reputation as one of the most dangerous taverns in London. It was notorious for its 'posture girls' i.e. strippers! The tavern was demolished in 1766 and the site is now covered by the Theatre Royal, Drury Lane.

Hogarth's A Rake's Progress; shows Tom Rakewell in the Rose Tavern, on Drury Lane, being relieved of his pocket watch by two women. Behind them a group of figures sit drinking, whilst a woman removes her clothes in the foreground. To the right a waiter is seen entering with a street singer.

Rules Restaurant

This is the oldest surviving restaurant in London, dating back to 1798. It was established by Thomas Rule, when it was noted for its "porter, pies and oysters" being traditional English fare.

It has long been a favourite with numerous distinguished people; Charles Dickens, H.G. Wells and Thackeray dined here as did Bertie the Prince of Wales, Queen Victoria's eldest son, later to become Edward VII, with the actress Lily Langtry. A special door was made for the couple so that they could enter and leave without being seen and they wined and dined in a private curtained alcove on the first floor.

Lily Langtry

A special door was made for the couple so that they could enter and leave without being seen...

Rules Restaurant

Bertie, Queen Victoria's eldest son was a regular patron of Rules restaurant

Notable Pubs and Clubs - continued
Covent Garden was and is still famous for its hospitality...

Casanova is known to have visited the Shakespeare's Head

The Shakespeare's Head

Another notorious tavern, in the northeast corner of Covent Garden, next to the entrance of the Covent Garden Theatre (now the Royal Opera House). Among its famous customers were the biographer James Boswell and the flamboyant young spendthrift William Hickey. In 1763, The Shakespeare's Head was visited by the Italian adventurer and womaniser Casanova. Although many prostitutes were procured for him, he apparently declined them all.

The Garrick Club

The Duke of Sussex founded the club in 1831 mainly for actors, painters and other followers of the arts. The club first met in a hotel in King St but the present meeting place is a building in Garrick St designed by Frederick Marrable in 1864. The club was named after the actor David Garrick (who lived briefly in nearby King Street) and it owns a large collection of fine paintings, including portraits by Kneller and Lely, bought from the comedian Charles Mathews who was an early member. Members have included Dukes, Earls, Barons and notable writers such as Dickens and Thackeray. Its membership nowadays is made up of people connected to theatre, television and media arts, publishers, writers and lawyers.

The Coach and Horses

This tavern in Wellington Street dates back to the 1730s and was one of the first to advertise 'always something to eat'. It is now well-known for salt beef and draught Guinness.

The Garricks Head

It was here, in Bow Street, that the infamous 'Judge and Jury' mock trials were staged by 'judge' Baron Nicholson. Cases, usually lewd and bawdy, were acted out and heard,

Exterior of the Garrick Club. Watercolour, pen and brown ink, by Frederick Marrable (1818-72), c.1863

then sentences decided following much obscenity and consumption of alcohol. Women were not allowed in till around midnight so any female 'witnesses' were played by men in drag.

Freemasons' Hall

The Freemasons have had their English headquarters in Great Queen Street since 1717. They would at first meet in many of the halls and taverns in the area but the first permanent lodge opened in 1776. The present Freemasons' Hall dates from 1933, a building with a magnificent interior incorporating a library and museum exhibiting memorabilia from the last three hundred years and which is often used in television and film dramas, for example doubling as the MI5 building in the BBC's *Spooks* series.

Freemasons come from all walks of British life and all have in common a moral code of brotherhood and charitable benevolence.

Freemasons' Hall

The Cyder Cellars

These were opened in Maiden Lane in 1730 and were famous for their musical evenings. The Victorian novelist William Thackeray drank here, describing the varied and vibrant fellow customers thus: *"healthy country tradesmen and farmers in London for their business, came and recreated themselves with the jolly singing and suppers at the Back Kitchen; squads of young apprentices, dashing young medical students, young University bucks, handsome young guardsmen and florid bucks"*.

Handbill for the Cyder Cellars

Over hundreds of years, the name 'Savoy' has been given to a palace, a chapel, a hotel and a theatre, in addition to several streets off the Strand.

These all have their beginnings on the site of land granted by Henry III in 1246 to Peter, Earl of Richmond, the uncle of his Queen, Eleanor. Peter later became Count of Savoy and had Simon de Montfort build a grand palace on the land, deemed to be "the fayrest mannor in Europe". Peter died in 1263 and bequeathed the palace to the monastery of Great St. Bernard at Montjeux in Savoie but Queen Eleanor bought it back in 1270 for her second son, Edmund, Earl of Lancaster. The French King John stayed there in 1357 when he was a captive of the Black Prince, and six years later returned of his own free will to stay until he died on 9th April 1364. It eventually passed down in 1361 to John of Gaunt, Duke of Lancaster, who proved very unpopular, and during the Peasants' Revolt in 1381 was burnt down by Wat Tyler's followers. The Duke survived, although some of his servants were executed. Members of the mob were themselves killed when the wine cellar in which they were drinking the Duke's wine, fell in and trapped them.

The palace was virtually derelict until Henry VII ordered it to be rebuilt in 1505 as a hospital for the poor dedicated to St. John the Baptist. It contained three chapels, including 'The Savoy Chapel'. The hospital was used variously as a refuge for wounded soldiers and sailors, as a military prison and as a Jesuit school for boys. The buildings gradually deteriorated and in 1864, a fire left only the walls of the Savoy Chapel standing.

The Savoy Theatre

Designed by C.J. Phipps it was founded in 1881 by Richard D'Oyly Carte for the production of Gilbert and Sullivan's operas. It was the first public building in London to have electric lighting. Many Gilbert and Sullivan operas were performed here including *The Mikado* and *The Gondoliers* but the partnership broke up in the 1890s when Gilbert and D'Oyly Carte argued over expenses. Since then, there have been numerous successful and long-running plays put on here, such as William Douglas-Home's *The Secretary Bird* and Michael Frayn's *Noises Off*, which ran for 1,912 performances. The theatre was completely rebuilt and redecorated in 1929.

The Savoy from an 1851 drawing

The Savoy Chapel

The original chapel in the palace of John of Gaunt was destroyed with the rest of the building in the Peasants' Revolt of 1381. When the Savoy was rebuilt in 1505 as a hospital for the poor, a new chapel was dedicated to St. John the Baptist in 1510. The fire of 1864 left only the outside walls so Sydney Smirke carried out restoration work in 1864-5. By the 1880s the chapel had become popular with the upper classes as a desirable place for weddings. It was the first place of worship to have electricity in 1890 and in 1937 it became the Chapel of the Royal Victorian Order. When it was refitted in 1939, it was re-titled the King's Chapel of the Savoy and is now of course, the Queen's Chapel of the Savoy.

The Queen's Chapel of the Savoy

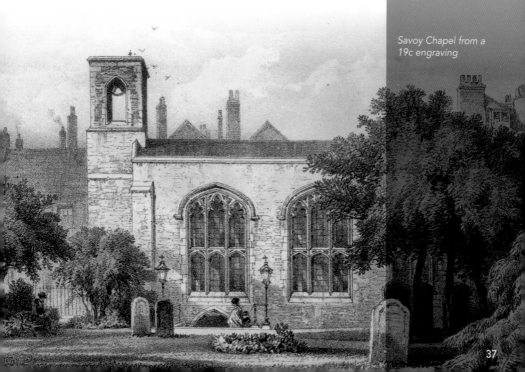

Savoy Chapel from a 19c engraving

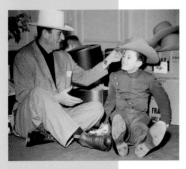

The Savoy Hotel

The hotel was another development devised by Richard D'Oyly Carte, next to his Savoy Theatre. It opened on 6th August 1889 and another block was added in 1903-4. The most innovative hotel of its time, it was one of the first London hotels to incorporate full electric lighting, lifts and hot and cold running water, and was remarkable for having 67 bathrooms!

Cesar Ritz came from Monte Carlo to open the Savoy Restaurant and Auguste Escoffier was one of the first chefs. The hotel became renowned for its impeccable service and attention to detail and many rich and famous people held sparkling, champagne-filled parties. An American, Harry Rosenfeld from Chicago, used the first sovereign to pay for a bottle of *Moët et Chandon* champagne at the Savoy and the coin is on display in the Savoy Museum. Sumptuous creative dishes were invented including *Pêches Melba* in honour of Dame Nellie Melba, the opera singer, and an omelette made with smoked haddock for the novelist Arnold Bennett which is still served in the Savoy Grill today. Others were created for the likes of Lily Langtree, the Prince of Wales, later to be Edward VII, and Sarah Bernhardt, the actress.

One of the most opulent parties was the famous Gondola Dinner, hosted by a Wall St financier, George Kessler. He entertained his guests in a recreated Venice in the old courtyard which was made watertight and flooded to a depth of 4 ft. Scenery was erected on the walls and the centrepiece was a large silk-lined gondola decorated with 12,000 fresh carnations, in which the guests were seated. There was a baby elephant, a 5 ft birthday cake and the tenor Caruso was there as a singing gondolier. Four hundred Venetian lamps lit the area.

From top: Marilyn Monroe & Laurence Olivier, 1956

John Wayne and a Savoy page boy, trying on stetsons, 1950s

Below: Gene Autry and Champion in the Lancaster Room, 1953

Patronised by Royalty, Maharajahs, leading stars and impresarios alike, the Savoy became renowned for its British style and tradition coupled with innovation. In 1893 the American Bar was one of the first to serve 'American' cocktails. Yet despite the innovative interior, Savoy Court, leading to the Strand entrance to the Savoy, is the only street in the British Isles where traffic must keep to the right! The Savoy Grill, established in the 1890s, remains today one of the best hotel restaurants in London. In 1923 the two Savoy dance bands, the *Savoy Orpheans* and the *Savoy Havana Band* became the first to broadcast dance music from the Ballroom. Gershwin gave the first London performance of *Rhapsody in Blue* in the Savoy Ballroom and the Prima Ballerina Anna Pavlova first danced in cabaret at the Savoy.

The Savoy - continued
"The fayrest mannor in Europe"

Exterior of the Savoy Hotel and Theatre from Exeter Street in the 1900s

The artist Claude Monet stayed three times at the Savoy from 1899, painting the Thames from his room on the fifth floor, seeking to catch it in all weather and light conditions. Winston Churchill visited the Savoy every week when he was in London and in 1953, when Queen Elizabeth II's Coronation Ball was held at the Savoy, he brought the Pasha of Marrakech to see the wonderful hotel decorations. The late actor Richard Harris, star of *Camelot* and the *Harry Potter* films, lived in the Savoy whilst in London until his death in 2002, and according to a report from the hotel's archivist, his words as he was leaving on a stretcher were *"It was the food!"*

The hotel closed in December 2007 for extensive refurbishment and 3,000 of its famous furnishings and memorabilia were auctioned. It is now managed by Fairmont Hotels and Resorts and has been modernized but the period style décor blends the old and the new with stunning Edwardian and Art Deco style interiors. The hotel was reopened by Charles, Prince of Wales in October 2010.

HRH Prince and Princess of Wales at the Savoy c.1984

The Savoy Winter Garden (circa 1906 -1910)

THE
HOUSE OF THE
ROYAL SOCIETY FOR
THE ENCOURAGEMENT
OF ARTS MANUFACTURES
AND COMMERCE'
FOUNDATION LAID 28 MARCH 1772
COMPLETED 24 APRIL 1774
ROBERT & JAMES ADAM
ARCHITECTS

A small district which includes the Adelphi Terrace, Robert Street and John Adam Street, was named after the Adelphi Buildings, which were built in 1768-72 by the renowned Scottish architects, the Adam brothers.

The glamorous development by the ambitious brothers, John, Robert, James and William, was at the centre of 18th century coffee house society, consisting of a huge precinct of neo-classical houses which stood on the land between the River Thames and the Strand. They were arranged with the grandest terrace of all overlooking the river; this was called 'Royal Terrace', later known as 'Adelphi Terrace'. Although most of the buildings were demolished in the 1930s amid much controversy, a remaining example, now the home of the Royal Society of Arts, can be seen in John Adam Street. Among the famous residents of this prestigious estate were David Garrick, Richard D'oyley Carte, Thomas Hardy and George Bernard Shaw.

Above: RSA commemorative plaque

The 1772 home of Royal Society of Arts in John Adam Street

Adelphi Terrace from a 19c engraving. The site is now occupied by the 1936-8 Grade II listed Art Deco 'New Alelphi Building', by Colcutt and Hamp

Sainsbury's built up a reputation for exceptionally high standards of cleanliness and food hygiene. With its modern, innovative approach, it became a significant business by the 1920s and today, continues to expand.

1869: Sainsbury's first shop at 173 Drury Lane

Apart from the market traders, many famous retailers began in Covent Garden. One of the best known is the firm of Moss Bros. Moses Moses opened a shop in Bedford St in 1860, selling second-hand clothes.

His two sons, Alfred and George, opened a similar shop in King Street and by 1917 had expanded to occupy a large corner site. Their speciality remains the hiring out of dress suits for all occasions, including weddings and coronations.

Sainsbury's supermarket had its modest beginnings in Covent Garden. Founded by John Sainsbury at 173 Drury Lane in 1869, with a shop selling dairy products, the business quickly prospered and other branches in London followed.

The famous auctioneers, Sotheby's, began here as a book-selling business founded by Samuel Baker in 1744. By 1754, Baker had opened sale rooms in Yorke St (now Tavistock St) dealing in books, manuscripts and prints. His nephew John Sotheby inherited the business and became renowned as a fine art auctioneers and valuers. The firm today has its premises in New Bond St.

The Lady magazine established in 1885 by Thomas Gibson Bowles, maternal grandfather of the Mitford sisters, has its offices at 39-40 Bedford St.

Stanfords, the largest map and travel guide retailer in the world, was founded in Long Acre in the 1800s. Long Acre was a centre for coach making, and when automobiles replaced horsepower the services changed. It was here that the Merryweather factory made London's

fire engines for 213 years up until the 1950s.

The most well known print works was Odhams Press, founded in 1894 in Floral St by the Odhams brothers. Their manager, Julius Salter Elias, realised the value of regular magazine work and consequently many publications such as Vanity Fair and Racing Pigeon were printed in Floral St. The firm moved to Long Acre in 1906. They won the contract to print the extremely popular John Bull weekly magazine, and eventually bought the title. Other magazines followed such as Harper's Bazaar and Good Housekeeping; eventually the print-works moved to Watford but the Covent Garden works are remembered today by Odhams Walk which is found between Long Acre and Neal St.

Neal's Yard is a place renowned for high-class foods. Housed in 19th century former warehouses are purveyors of fine cheeses, breads and salads. The old hoisting mechanisms can still be seen on their walls.

Neals Yard

Moss Bros' King Street premises

1901 Merryweather horse-drawn steam fire appliance

> *Little nips of whisky, little drops of gin, Make a lady wonder where on earth she's bin*
>
> Anon

Frontispiece and title page of 1773 edition of Harris's List

High class, fashionable Covent Garden went into decline in the 1700s, becoming notorious as a prostitution area. Prostitutes were known as 'Covent Garden nuns' and a 'Covent Garden ague' was a venereal disease!

Many of the prostitutes were naïve young girls who had come to the area looking for work in the theatre. While they waited for their big break, they stayed in 'boarding houses' run by dishonourable madams. They became 'ladies of pleasure' when they had to begin paying for their keep.

Harris's List

From 1757, for around thirty-eight years, a publication called *Harris's List of Covent Garden Ladies* was produced, a catalogue of up-market prostitutes describing all the physical attributes of each 'lady' together with her personality, sexual specialities and her charges. The name 'Harris' refers to Jack Harris, the head waiter of the Shakespeare's Head; he called himself the 'Pimp General of All England'. Visiting the 'handmaidens of love' was seen to be a gentlemanly pastime and Harris had a subscription of over 8000, many of whom were men of wealth and reputation.

Two neighbouring districts of equal infamy were those of St. Giles and Seven Dials. St. Giles was developed by Sir Thomas Neale, Master of the Mint, in the 17th century. He intended it to be a desirable area, but unfortunately, the wealthy preferred living in the West End of London leaving the houses to be occupied by the poorest families, often Irish immigrants, living in appalling slum conditions.

Left: Cheap Fish of St. Giles. From 'Street Life in London', by journalists J. Thomson and Adolphe Smith 1877-78

Right: The Crawlers. "Huddled together on the workhouse steps in Short's Gardens, those wrecks of humanity, the Crawlers of St. Giles's, may be seen both day and night seeking mutual warmth and mutual consolation in their extreme misery." From 'Street Life in London', by journalists J. Thomson and Adolphe Smith 1877-78

The whole of London was hit by a craze for gin drinking in the 1700s. St. Giles and Seven Dials were particularly badly affected. 18th century gin was nothing like today's gin. It was originally imported from Holland having been developed as a medicine produced by the distillation of white grain with juniper added for flavour.

In Holland in the 1580s, British troops fighting against the Spanish in the Dutch War of Independence, were given gin as 'Dutch Courage'. The people of London had long favoured beer because it was safer to drink than water and were not used to drinking spirits; consequently, they got drunk very quickly on what they called, 'Madam Jenever' escaping their miserable lives for a short time.

When the Government relaxed the law on distilling, Covent Garden became full of gin shops. The gin, made from very poor quality grain and often flavoured with turpentine, was so cheap that abuse of the drink became out of control. If you couldn't afford a glass, you could buy a gin-soaked rag! Notices were put up everywhere advertising, "Drunk for a penny, Dead drunk for tuppence, Straw for nothing"! In the 1730s, gin-fuelled crime was rife. One particular sad story tells of Judith Defor, a poor woman whose child was being cared for in the local workhouse. She took the child out one Sunday, strangled it and sold its clothes to pay for gin.

William Hogarth's famous engraving 'Gin Lane' is set in the St. Giles slums. It depicts the depravity unleased by addiction to gin; a half-naked drunken woman with syphillitic sores on her legs is shown failing to notice that her child is falling to its death amidst a scene of idleness and degradation. In 1751 The Tippling Act banned small gin shops, leaving the distribution of gin to larger retailers and distillers. This brought about a marked decline in gin drinking for a time but by the mid 19th century, consumption had again risen in Covent Garden. 'Gin palaces' first appeared around 1830; designed to be an escape from the filthy slums of the poor gin drinkers, they had luxurious interiors with grand furnishings.

Charles Dickens, who had come to Covent Garden to work in a blacking factory in Chandos Place under a supervisor called Bob Fagin, described the conditions in his 'Sketches by Boz', published in 1835:

"The gin-shops in and near Drury-Lane, Holborn, St. Giles's, Covent-garden, and Clare-market, are the handsomest in London. There is more filth and squalid misery near those great thoroughfares than in any part of this mighty city."

Charles Dickens

Indecency. A cartoon by the Scottish caricaturist Isaac Cruikshank (1756-1811) showing a woman urinating in the street, and saying: "B-t you, what are you stareing at?"

The night mayor. Alderman Wood, followed by constables, enters a thieve's kitchen where a watchman drinks gin with companions. Some figures escape through a door whilst a man trying to hide, upsets a woman on a chair.

The replica Seven Dials pillar was erected in 1989

Gin rendered men impotent, women sterile and was a major reason why the death rate in 1730s London exceeded that of the birth rate

With the situation worsening by the 19th century, St. Giles had become known as 'the Rookery' with professional criminals living in the decaying buildings, teaching children to become pickpockets or prostitutes. Mother Cummings was one example; she trained young prostitutes to entice drunken men to her home where they were then robbed.

The houses were packed from cellar to attic with people and children; the cellars were entered through trap-doors in the pavement and were sqalid dark holes with no running water or sanitation. A 'St. Giles cellar' epitomized the lowest possible type of accommodation.

Like St. Giles, Seven Dials was also instigated by Thomas Neale in 1693. It was built at the junction of seven streets, with a Doric pillar at the centre supporting six sundials. The original pillar was removed in 1773 when it was mistakenly thought that a large sum of money was hidden in the base; it still survives in Weybridge, Surrey where it was re-erected in 1882 in honour of Frederica, Duchess of York. A replica was put up in Seven Dials in 1989.

Far from being an attractive place to live, Seven Dials too became a meeting place for the poorest street-hawkers, villains and thieves.

William Hogarth's *Gin Lane*

Amidst the squalor of 19th century Covent Garden, several institutions helped those in need. Endell Street, for example, was built specifically for impoverished Londoners and was named after a Parish Rector, James Endell Taylor, who had devoted his life to defending the rights of the poor.

Here, a washhouse and a public bath house were built in 1853, funded by the Parish of St. Giles where the poor unwashed could go to make themselves clean.

Next to the bath house was the Borough of Holborn Workhouse which offered a roof over the head and food to eat to the destitute. The inmates came from all walks of life; they included the elderly, orphans, disabled and unmarried mothers. All were expected to work for their keep and had to give up their right to vote.

St. Giles National Schools opened in Endell Street in 1859, funded by the parish and designed by E.M. Barry. Boys and girls of poor families would have been the first generation to have had any formal education. On the first day, 900 pupils attended, but the playground was only 40 square feet (12 square metres)! The school continued until 1963.

The main housing for the poor was in Drury Lane and Bedfordbury, provided by Peabody and the 'Society for Improving the Conditions of the Labouring Classes'. The conditions were extremely miserable,

with whole families to one room. Much of the slum area was cleared away when Charing Cross Road and Shaftesbury Avenue were built in the 1880s, and it is now as it was intended, an appealing, vibrant area full of specialist shops and restaurants.

The former St Giles National Schools building in Endell Street

The Bow Street Runners
A response to crime

The original Bow Street was built in the 1630s in the shape of a bow, running between Floral Street and Tavistock Street. Although Bow Street was a place of high quality housing and shops, where many celebrated people lived including Grinling Gibbons the woodcarver and Charles Macklin the actor, it was also a haunt for criminals, becoming known as 'Thieving Alley'.

The Bow Street Magistrates Court was set up in 1740 by Thomas de Veil at No. 4. Henry Fielding, a lawyer and novelist, became the second Bow St. magistrate. In response to the increasing crime and disorder caused by the brothels and gin houses of Covent Garden and the apparent incompetence of the parish watchmen and constables, Fielding

Artist's depiction of the Bow Street Runners in action

Bow Street Magistrates'
Court as drawn by
Augustus Pugin and
Thomas Rowlandson
for Ackerman's
'Microcosm of London'
(1808-11)

John Fielding

Henry Fielding

Far left:
John Townsend - a
well-known Bow Street
Runner

established in 1749, a team of six non-uniformed volunteer 'thief-takers'. These became known as the Bow St Runners in 1754, when Henry's blind half-brother John took over as magistrate. He brought about schemes for helping young prostitutes and homeless boys, getting them trained to work at sea. He also pushed for magistrates to be paid, in order to avoid bribery, although this wasn't introduced until 1792. At first the Runners were part-time and could retain the money paid for convictions and private commissions, but corruption amongst them and magistrates soon became rife.

The Bow St. Runners were eventually overtaken in 1828 by a new force introduced by Sir Robert Peel, the famous 'Peelers'. These were the forerunners of the Metropolitan Police, whose model was to spread gradually across the world.

Blue lamps were introduced outside police stations in 1861; however Queen Victoria was reminded of the blue room in which Prince Albert had died whenever she visited the Royal Opera House. She ordered that Bow Street should be the only police station to have a white lamp rather than blue.

The present magistrates court, designed by Sir John Taylor, was built between 1879 and 1881 on the eastern side of Bow St, incorporating a police station and police court.

Spooks of Covent Garden
Some of the inhabitants have never left...

Dan Leno

The vanishing Mme. Rachel

Willam Terriss whose last words were said to have been: "I will be back"

Covent Garden is one of the most haunted areas of London. For such a small area, it has been filled with scandal and roguish wrong-doings over hundreds of years and it is small wonder that some of its most colourful characters should return to haunt this fascinating area.

Among the phantoms to appear are some made famous by the theatre:

The Adelphi is said to be haunted by the phantom of the murdered actor William Terriss; during the Edwardian era the ghost of a very tall man with white gloves, a trademark of Terriss, was seen but nobody was able to see his face until a staff member came face to face with the ghost in a corridor in 1950. When the likeness was compared with old pictures of actors, it was decided that the apparition was indeed the actor beloved by the

Victorians. His ghost is also said to have been seen at Covent Garden Tube Station, where before its construction, a bakery stood that he had visited faithfully every morning until his death. It has also been suggested that he haunts the Lyceum Theatre; here the spectre of a male corpse appears, with a grey appearance, loudly weeping in grief and sorrowful lament.

The Lyceum has several resident ghosts; Madame Tussaud who opened her first waxworks collection here appears, cradling the head of a man in her arms. Manifestations of the actress Ellen Terry have been seen waving in the gallery before abruptly vanishing.

There is said to be a resident ghost at the Garrick Theatre; a former tenant who rented a top floor flat directly off the stage, has apparently at times tapped performers' shoulders for good luck.

At the Theatre Royal, Drury Lane, a phantom 'man in grey' is said to appear, during long runs at the theatre, to people during daylight hours. He is richly dressed as an 18th century nobleman with a grey jacket, lacy shirt and high riding boots. Whilst undertaking various refurbishments of the building in 1870, workmen uncovered a skeleton with a dagger in the chest. The fragments of clothing found on the skeleton were made of grey cloth.

CITY OF WESTMINSTER

WILLIAM TERRISS
1847 - 1897
HERO OF THE ADELPHI
MELODRAMAS
MET HIS UNTIMELY END
OUTSIDE THIS THEATRE
10 DEC 1897

THE ADELPHI THEATRE CO. LTD

There have also been sightings of the famous comedian Dan Leno who began his career as a clog dancer and went on to appear in the Theatre Royal pantomime every year from 1888 until he died in 1904. The great clown Joseph Grimaldi performed here many times; he was known to be a good-natured fellow who liked to help young aspiring actors. Since his death, many nervous inexperienced novices have felt his guiding hands on their shoulders comforting and calming them so that they were able to give good performances.

After his death,
sightings began of a
tall, thin, ugly ghost
in the theatre's pit

In 1735 the actor Charles Macklin, a tall, lanky and unattractive man, killed a fellow actor during an argument by forcing a cane through the man's left eye into his brain. Despite there being witnesses, Macklin got away with the murder and lived to the great age of 107. After his death, sightings began of a tall, thin, ugly ghost in the theatre's pit.

Away from the theatres, many of the Covent Garden streets have been the focus of ghostly apparitions. Samuel Pepys, who lived and wrote his diaries at 12 Buckingham Street has been seen at that property's window, smiling down at passers-by. At number 14 of the same street, a young woman, thought to be Mme Rachel, a model of the artist William Etty in the 1840s, peers from her window, smiling flirtatiously, then slowly vanishes.

Anne Boleyn's ghost may be seen on Durham House Street; when she was charged with witchcraft and incest following her failure to bear Henry VIII an heir, she spent her last miserable months at Durham House before being taken to the tower for execution. Although the house no longer stands, the cellars remain and it is here that her ghostly form wanders aimlessly, dressed in a crimson gown, displaying her characteristic long neck and eleven fingers.

Among many more, the ghost of a poor prostitute, Jenny, who was murdered in Robert Street while trying to rob a customer, appears as a hunched, rag-covered body. Those who are walking in the 'Jenny's Hole' area may hear the murder with sounds of a struggle and echoing screams before a chilling silence ensues.

A ghostly Samuel
Pepys peers out from
12 Buckingham Street

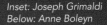

Inset: Joseph Grimaldi
Below: Anne Boleyn

A Few Street Facts
Many streets have famous associations

Orange Street – part of the street was built in the 1690s on the site of stables owned by James Scott, Duke of Monmouth. The Protestant Duke was executed following the battle of Sedgemoor in 1685; he was taken at the age of 36 for beheading by the infamous inefficient and brutal Jack Ketch on Tower Hill. Ketch wielded several blows of the axe before resorting to a knife to finish the job. When Monmouth's body was taken to the Tower, it was realized that there were no official paintings of him so it was decided that the artist William Wissing should do a portrait. The Royal Surgeon had to hurriedly stitch his head back on to his body and tie a white cravat round the neck! Wissing had 24 hours to complete the painting before the body deteriorated; the portrait can still be seen in the National Portrait Gallery.

James Scott, Duke of Monmouth

My Fair Lady was set in and around James St

Charles Dickens is thought to have based his 'Old Curiosity Shop' on one of the buildings in Orange Street.

James Street – the 1964 film *My Fair Lady* recreates James Street in the scenes where Eliza Doolittle walks along singing *Wouldn't it be loverly* and where her father sings *I'm getting married in the morning.*

Cecil Court

Cecil Court – was named after Robert Cecil, the first Earl of Salisbury and dates back to the 17th century. In 1764 the young composer Wolfgang Amadeus Mozart and his family came to live here while the eight year old boy was touring Europe.

England's first successful identikit prosecution resulted from a murder committed in Cecil Court. When in March 1961, an elderly shop worker was found dying from stab wounds following a botched robbery at no. 23, an identikit picture of the attacker was circulated amongst the police and local press. A police officer on the beat spotted the similarity between the identikit and a man called Edwin Bush whose shoe prints matched those at the crime scene. A local shopkeeper supplied further evidence saying that Bush had tried to sell him a sword which had been stolen in the robbery; Bush was tried and executed the same year.

Denmark Street is London's 'Tin Pan Alley', always associated with music. It originated in the 1800s when most of the buildings housed sheet music publishers and suppliers to the orchestras of the nearby theatres and music halls.

Recording studios were set up in the 1960s; the Rolling Stones recorded their first album at Regent Sounds Studio, 4 Denmark Street, followed by many others including the Kinks, Stevie Wonder and Jimi Hendrix. Musicians still visit the specialist music shops of this renowned area of rock and roll history. Bob Marley is said to have bought his first ever guitar here and other celebrity visitors include Paul McCartney, David Bowie, Eric Clapton and Noel Gallagher.

Chandos Place was named after the wife of the fourth Earl of Bedford, Catherine Brydges of Chandos, and was the scene of the capture of the notorious highwayman Claude Duval. It was while he was at The Hole in the Wall Tavern drunkenly boasting of his exploits to the admiring females who thought him dashing and romantic, that he was caught. He was subsequently hanged and buried in St. Paul's Church, Covent Garden. It was in Chandos Place that Charles Dickens learnt how to survive as an

impoverished boy in London. Both his parents had been jailed for debt and in 1823, in order to feed himself, young Charles had to begin work sticking labels onto pots of boot polish in a factory on Chandos Place. He worked under the supervision of a man called Bob Fagin, earning just enough for food and drink and later described the factory in his memoirs, "A crazy, tumbledown old house literally overrun with rats".

Henrietta Street was named after Charles I's wife Henrietta Maria. Jane Austen lodged at number 10 when she visited her London publishers.

Alfred Hitchcock set his film *Frenzy* in Covent Garden; his evil character Bob Rusk carried out his villainous acts of murder and rape in a flat at 3 Henrietta Street and is seen heaving a body bag onto a market wagon full of potatoes.

Regent Sounds Studios where the Rolling Stones recorded their first album

Bob Marley is said to have bought his first ever guitar here

Jane Austen

Henrietta Street

Acknowledgements

Rita Greer Des RCA, MUniv.
Having some ancestral connections with Covent Garden, Rita, born in 1942, has had an illustrious career in the arts. Graduating from the Royal College of Art as a craftsman-jeweller in 1965, this occupation kept her gainfully employed until the 1970s. Between 1980 and 2000 she worked in industry engaged in graphics, illustration, packaging and TV commercials. After 'retiring' in 2002 she chose to specialize in the painting of historical figures and events. Made an Honorary Master of the Open University in 2010 for her 'notable contribution to education and culture' Rita has had over 30 books published, all to help people. We are extremely grateful to Rita for creating original artworks specially for this book. Others used are reproduced under Free Art License v1.3 which applies only to those images specified on page 56. (For more of Rita's work see Wikimedia/Rita Greer/Robert Hooke/Commons).

And for providing invaluable help and assistance in the production of this book, our thanks go to:

Covent Garden Area Trust. A registered charity with between 12 and 22 trustees set up in 1988 to conserve the historic architecture, environment and special, unique qualities of the 97-acre Covent Garden area – www.cgareatrust.org.uk

Covent Garden Community Association *Founded in 1971 in response to the GLC's disastrous plans to redevelop the area. After a long and bitter struggle these plans were defeated and Covent Garden was saved from the bulldozers.* www.coventgarden.org.uk

London Transport Museum – www.ltmuseum.co.uk

Chris Buckley, The Lamb and Flag – www.lambandflagcoventgarden.co.uk

In and Around Covent Garden – www.coventgarden.uk.com

The Savoy Hotel – www.fairmont.com/savoy-london

The Theatres Trust Image Library – www.theatrestrust.org.uk.

Nicole Leggett, Sister-PR – www.sisteris.com

Grace's Guide – www.GracesGuide.co.uk

Pre-Construct Archaeology – www.pre-construct.com

AOC Archaeology Group – www.aocarchaeology.com

Barry Stewart, The Royal Opera House – www.roh.org.uk

Tony Reading – www.covent-garden.co.uk

Frank To – www.franktofienart.com www.facebook.com/FrankToFineArtist
– www.bbc.co.uk/news/uk-scotland-12934050

Eleanor Godley *editorial* research **Laura Godley** pencil sketches page 50

Covent Garden Piazza by Wenceslaus Hollar (1607-1677)

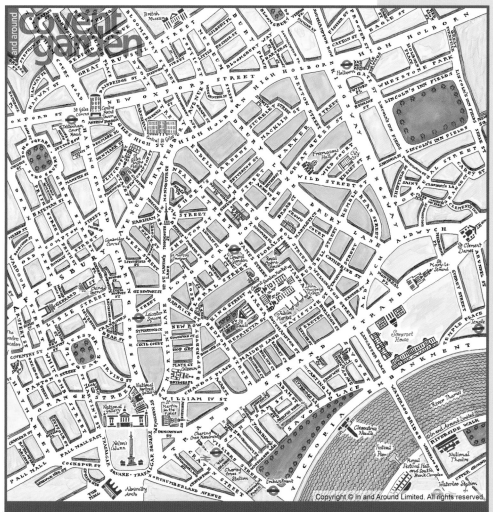

In and Around Covent Garden

is the only membership organisation dedicated to the promotion of the Covent Garden area and the businesses within it. We promote the area in a number of ways including:

- publishing the free monthly **In and Around Covent Garden** magazine

- publishing the Covent Garden website

- organising monthly networking events and additional social events

- organising Covent Garden Business Forum meetings

- acting as the voice of the Covent Garden community in liaison with a number of influential organisations impacting on the area

Save the Jubilee Hall – *Chuck Anderson with Ray Green*
Covent Garden Past – *John Richardson*
Walking Literary London – *Roger Tagholm*
Walking Notorious London – *Andrew Duncan*
Churches & Cathedrals of London – *Stephen Humphrey*
The Rebirth of Covent Garden – *Greater London Council*
Museum of London – *V. Cumming, N. Merriman, C. Ross*
Saxon and Norman London – *John Clark*
The London Encyclopaedia – *Ben Weinreb and Christopher Hibbert*
In and Around Covent Garden – *business and community development organisation*
The History of Gin (and Tonic) – *bbc.co.uk*
The Gin and Vodka website – *www.ginvodka.org*
The Really Useful Group Theatres *www.reallyuseful.com*
Monograph 2, Tatberht's Lundenwic – *Jim Leary, PCA Archaeology*
The Coffee Houses of Augustan London – *John D. Pelzer, History Today Magazine*
London Theatre Direct Ltd – *www.londontheatredirect.com*
Covent Garden – *its Romance and History* – *Reginald Jacobs*
London Under London – *R. Trench and E. Hillman*
The Thieves' Opera – *Lucy Moore*
Old and New London – *Cassel & Co*
Cassell's Illustrated History of England, 1865 – *Cassel & Co*
Lost London – *English Heritage*
Covent Garden Life – *www.coventgardenlife.com*
Life in a 17th Century Coffee Shop – *David Brandon*
www.postalheritage.wordpress.com

Images:
Many of the images are from the authors' collection or were photographed by them. Others were sourced from the following organisations:
Cover image: View of Covent Garden, Joseph Van Aken c1700-49, Bridgeman Art Library. Page 4, Beehive, Tatberht images/bone diagrams: Pre-Construct Archaeology. The Saxon brooch: © AOC Archaeology. Page 5, two St Martin's Courtyard images: Sister PR, © Andy Chopping, Museum of London Archaeology. Saxon burial and cremation vessels: © AOC Archaeology. Skeleton and antler working: © Pre-Construct Archaeology. Page 6, Francis, 4th Earl of Bedford and John Russell 1st Earl of Bedford; Rita Greer, Page 8, Inigo Jones: © Science Photo Library, Oliver Cromwell: Rita Greer. Page 9, The Great Plague: Rita Greer, Free Art License v1.3. Plague doctor: Frank To. Page 10, 1820's flower sellers: The Bishopsgate Institute. Page 11, Covent Garden Market by Balthazar Nebot: © City of London. Page 13, London Transport Museum Horse-drawn tram: © Andy Paradise, main busses and exterior: © Diane Auckland Fotohaus. Page 16, Interior of St. Clement Danes and aerial shot: © Izabella Seabrook. Page 20, Charles II: Rita Greer Free Art License v1.3, Sarah Siddons: Rita Greer. Page 21, Nell Gwynne: Rita Greer, exterior of Drury Lane Theatre in 1905: The Theatres Trust Image Library. Page 22 & 23, two tour images: Pete Le May, the backstage image: Sim Canetty-Clarke. Page 25, The Duchess Theatre: © Tony Reading. Page 26, The Garrick Theatre, 1902 and the façade of the Adelphi Theatre: The Theatres Trust Image Library, the Donmar Warehouse: © Tony Reading. Page 29, 17c coffee House, both oil on board: Rita Greer Free Art License v1.3, Page 30, Robert Hooke and Samuel Pepys: Rita Greer Free Art License v1.3. Page 32 Lamb and Flag, Chris Buckley, Page 33, Liliy Langtry: Rita Greer. Page 34, Casanova: Rita Greer, exterior of the Garrick Club: The Art Archive / Garrick Club Page 35, Cyder Cellars: Look and Learn. Page 38, all images: The Savoy Hotel. Page 40, Exterior of the Savoy Hotel and theatre: The Theatres Trust Image Library, winter garden and Their Royal Highnesses: The Savoy. Page 42 Sainsbury's exterior: © The Sainsbury Archive, Museum of London. Page 43, Merryweather fire engine: www.GracesGuide.co.uk, Page 44 Crawlers and Cheap Fish: The Bishopsgate Institute. Page 45, Charles Dickens: Rita Greer, the 'Night Mayor': © City of London/LMA. Page 47 Skeletal man in gin shop: © Science Photo Library. Page 48, Bow Street Runners in action: © Look and Learn the Peter Jackson collection. Page 49, the two Fielding brothers, Rita Greer, Page 50 & 51 Dan Leno, and Mme. Rachel, pencil sketches by Laura Godley. Anne Boleyn and the ghost of Samuel Pepys: Rita Greer. Page 52 the Duke of Monmouth and Audrey Hepburn as Eliza Doolittle in 'My Fair Lady': Rita Greer. Page 53, Jane Austen: Rita Greer. Page 55, Page 55 map, In and Around Covent Garden.